Poems to Read Aloud

Poems to Read Aloud

by Aileen Mills

JM

JEREMY MILLS
PUBLISHING

Published by Jeremy Mills Publishing
Limited
The Red House, Occupation Road, Lindley,
Huddersfield HD3 3BD
www.jeremymillspublishing.co.uk

First Published 2004
© Aileen Mills

ISBN 0-9546484-3-9

A CIP catalogue record for this book is
available from the British Library.

Acknowledgements

Thanks to Harry, Diana, Brian, Jeremy and Iain.

Contents

Cat

After the manner of Christopher Smart

I tell of my cat Gussie
For she is special with me
And I am choice of her.
For her colours please me
She has cinnamon and black
And her white rivals blossom.

I tell of my cat Gussie
For she has modest roots
For she comes of a basket of kittens.
Her fragile mask
Has something of the East
For her eyes are slits
And then are brightest orbs.
For when she climbs upward she is an arrow
And downward a falling star.

I tell of my cat Gussie
For with her sharp claws
She is a mouser, birder, frogger
Yet her velvet paws
Will pat a humble bee

Or a face.
Then her name is Gossamer.

I tell of my cat Gussie
For she will bring trophies
To my shoe.
A coloured leaf,
An ill-formed twig,
A puff-ball,
A great green caterpillar
Of an errant moth
In gentle teeth.

Too early in her time
Came the ravisher
A tall traveller;
Three live kits
Were her reward
One, Mab stayed with her
Until she was blown away
On a bleak Christmas day.

I tell of my cat Gossamer
For every day to my shoes
She brings black socks
Supposing they are kittens.

My cat Gossamer
Is special with me
And I am choice of her.

Kitten

She was so sweet a pet,
So neat and fleet a pet,
That the heart lost a pace at the grace
Of the innocent face.
She was so sleek a pet,
Sometimes meek a pet,
Unique a pet,
From the pins in her velvet paws
To the nip of her fragile jaws.

She was a treasure, a pleasure
Without measure,
And might be so today,
Had not a wanton driver on a cold road
Blown her away.

Envoie:

I had not thought the world to be
Too small to hold both Mab and me.

In Memoriam
1894 - 1914

Charlie was born on the first day of April,
Never grew taller than four foot one.
His mother was sour as a rhubarb stalk
Her husband six years dead and gone.
When they said to her "Where did you get
such a son"?
Charlie's mother never let on.

He was so small it seems he hardly grew
Face bones long, his bowed limbs askew
Red feathers of hair, eyes moonstone blue.
And time went on with Sunday school
And day school, and playtime,
For this small holy fool.

And time went on and time went on
Summer a frolic of flowers in the warm night
"Jack o' the Green" and strawberries wild
and violets white;
Winter wind, dark and dank with scudding
cloud
Frost standing proud
Screech owls calling loud.

Charlie asked his mother one day
"Why am I different from another?
"When my head tells me I am the same?"
And she replied "You are a curse,
"An ill made mommet. You are my shame."
And still time spun his web.

Charlie moved out to a shed in the orchard.
"See me live with my creatures", he said,
As he gathered bracken to make his bed.
Belgian hares, grey as a badger,
A cage of ferrets, lissom and long as an adder;
Moleskins nailed to the frail door,
Brackets to hold the ladder
That boosted him to the reeded roof
Where his owlets posed aloof.

In a baccy tin in the ferrets cage
Were seven golden sovereigns, Charlie's
wage
For plucking turkeys Christmas time,
Unsexing kittens, gathering holly
Plaiting for the maidens now and then
A golden corn-straw dolly.
And time went on, and time went on.

Sometimes the village lads called him to ploys
Daft shoving about, silly village boys,

Not all good, not all bad,
Each a stupid village lad.
And one soft night in early June
Crazy with unfulfilled promise
And full of moon,
One put a noggin of gin in Charlie's cider
His laugh was a shout, his eyes gaped wider.
They said "Get the ladder and climb to the sky"
"Just the job" they heard him cry.
"I'm drunk as a fiddler's bitch"
"I'm drunk as a skunk"- he footed every rung.
At the top he hung
Charlie the curse, neither old nor young.

Time stopped its movement
"See me fly - see I'm flying now."
Charlie fell like a stone upon his head.
One cried out "Jesus! Is he dead?"
The boys scattered - all save one who sat
By Charlie through moonshine to the rising
of the sun.

Here Charlie lies within another bed
In the churchyard verge where the poorest lie
With only to mourn him one such as I.

On the day before her son was lapped in clay

Charlie's mother arose and went away.
One saw her pass the cider pound for higher
ground
The main road to other places.
He watched her pass in the warm June rain,
Charlie's mother was not seen again.

The cottage died, the village dreamed
And from a far-off place, a place too far
Came war. The mothers watched
The ploughboys from the frugal farms
Run to the bugles brass alarms
And fisher boys left the nets for the wild
waves
To prove that Britons never shall be slaves.
Loyal cheers and scalding tears
And the war went on - and time went on.

Of the four good bad village boys
Three, a triple loss
Names on a granite cross.
But one returned, scarred, burned
And shouted loud his pain in many a green
lane.
"There's rats under the breast bones
"Of men who lie down alone."
And raved of Vimy Ridge.

He found the sad cottage
He came on Charlie's orchard shed
Pushed at the rotten door
Stamped the cages into dust
The bones and fur to must.

Found the Capstan baccy tin
With seven golden sovereigns in,
"Medals", he roared, "Medals for the war",
And flung them to the brambles and the
weeds.
"There's three that died", he said, "And one
still bleeds.
"It matters not how many died or bled
"I won a war for you Charlie."
He said.

Early one morning....

We found the place by chance, I and Artemis
From the high moor, down a steep narrow lane,
Hedged with hazel bushes,
We came out upon a plain, a small plain.
And from that plain the town crawled up the hill.
There were fine shops, a library, a clock
tower
And a market hall.
We looked at them all.
"Where are the people?", I said.
"It's early yet", said Artemis.
So we ambled down again onto the plain.

There were three high houses, a farrier
And a small mill grinding grain for animal
feed
And on the door of one house
Was the legend "Women's Commune - Hand
made goods".
We pushed the door and mounted the dusty stair.
There were three rooms there.

In the first room there were pixy boots -
Hundreds of pairs, large as large, small as
small
In all colours, but mostly the colours of trees,

The browns and greens.
There were shoulder bags - hand bags.

In the second room there were tie-dyed
shirts,
Every tie a spreading flower,
And batik skirts,
There were scarves and shawls so cobweb
fine
They could be drawn through a wedding
ring.
There were tunics of amazing design and
frantic colour.

In the third room everything was white cotton -
Shifts in broderie, nightgowns frilled at the
neck
Large and small.
One shift so small that Artemis whispered
"It must be for a bridesmaid; this is wedding
stuff."
She turned it over, spoke aloud,
"This is labelled 'shroud'."

We stumbled downstairs on to the plain
again.
And strange, strange, there were women ev-
erywhere.

You could not count so many women,
Each with a push-chaired child,
Rugged bonneted, capped against the cold,
For it was a cold autumn day,
Bright as a meteor, cold as the moon.
We watched them as they walked
And heard the buzz of their talk
And Artemis said
"Listen - there's another sound
"Coming from the ground;
"There - listen - coming from the air."

So we listened and heard
A sound like the hum of bees,
Like the flight of birds with their dry pinions
Like the croon of a dove
With here and there a high note,
High as high, like the sound in a choir,
And all the time, this odd sound from ground
to air,
From air and higher
The sound of a choir.
And the women walked and the women
marched
And Artemis said
"You can hear birds winging,
"Listen, great heaven! The babies are sing-
ing."

We stood with closed eyes listening
How long? I cannot say, an hour?
Perhaps half a day,
And in the end we heard the music go gently
away
Till in the distance it was the hum and a
whistle
And a high note, fainter and fainter
We heard it go away.
We opened our eyes and there was no-one
there!
No woman, no push-chaired babies and now
no sound
But the clacking of the little mill
And the ring of the anvil.

And I said
"We must stay", but Artemis said
"No. We must make our way,
"We must go away during the day's gleam.
"Have you never heard of a waking dream?"

Early one morning,
We found the place by chance, Artemis and I
Down a slim lane to a small plain,
Which we never found again.

Dream

It was a bright day — bright, bright.
Now I am old and blind, all dreams are
bright.

I stood, my back to Fullers -
All marzipan and fondant cream
And smell of strong coffee.
On the pavement opposite, a man,
And between us the roadway of silent
streaming cars
Pastel blue, silver, rose and yellow
Nose to tail - inexorable, pale.

The man, spare, dark, small
Black haired and with a happy clown face,
Watching their pace,
He held out arms to me
I knew him
"Jokanaan!"
So high in warm regard,
Two generations gone, and the war had
claimed him.
"Come over to me" he said
"You'll love it over here."
I raised my hands too
And saw my hands were young.

"I cannot come."
"But why? None can want you
As much as I."
"I have children."
"Let your mother hold them
Love them, approve them."
"O Jokanaan!"
The silent cars surged onward
And he was drawn away into deep shadow.

I will dream that dream again
Defy the silent traffic
I will hold out my hands
And snatch at the hands of Jokanaan.

Sailor

You are the Mermaid's face.
At night, on watch I see your green
Drowned hair in the waves trough.

From the bowl of the sky
The stars sing out your little name,
The name your mother gave you.
She should have named you Eve or Lilith

Let me love you.
She turns her head to listen.
She did not know this word.
Her peers, the clumsy boys
Muttered "cool" and "fabulous" and "fantastic".

And this man, sculpted and smooth,
Spoke of mermaids and singing stars.
She lifts warm arms to hold him
And for all time disturbs her peace.

Sailor II

The boy musician made her a song,
He loved her sadly for he was young.
The lawyer offered heart and head,
"Kindest of men", but "no", she said.
The writer made her a story
She smiled but she turned away.
The traveller paused in his journey
And whispered "I am here to stay".
The curate held up his looking glass
"Beware", he said, "this soon will pass".

But a frigate came into the harbour,
Dressed overall for the fair
There was blue and gold and gold and blue
And the sailor standing there.
He took her hands into his hands
And drew her into his light.
He took her hands into his hands
And drew her into the night.

He brought her rows of shiny beads
And took her love for his fee
The he suddenly tore her joy apart
And the frigate and the sailor

Went back to the sea.

She saw them go with burning eyes
From the deep of a pain-racked paradise.

Sailor III

My English mother named me Ambrose
But I am not divine or lovely,
I am a stunted man,
Like Rufus in quadrato corpore,
Square with one eye brown and one eye grey.

In Sydney, Double Bay,
With a frangipani and peach tree, there is a
wife.
Tall as a tree, wide-hipped, large her hips
and hands:
Yet loving me.

Tall and broad one daughter. Then in ten
years
Dropped my little Ambrosine with such
brown eyes
That drew the lust of men
I in my freighter, master;
With goods for the good,
And on return a lighter of coal for Sydney.

In Newcastle, up the coast
Lives my comfort and my joy
My ease and my relief,
Six feet tall. Tall as a tree,

Wide hipped, with long slim hands and feet.
Then I am Ambrose,
Then I am divine and lovely.

Fisherman

He is at one
With the desert of water and skies,
The skyline ends the sight of his far away eyes.
He is lord of the nets and the orange floats.
A share for the master,
One for the crew
The third is the boat's.
He is a strong man
He is king of the wheel
Lord of the traps and lord of the creel.
When the catch is small
Is he servant of them all?

Radio Voices

"My name", she says, "is Amy Grace."
Speaking with soft gentility
To someone clad in headphones
And a tiger smile and verbal flexibility.
"Thank you sweetie, I'm all ears."
"My name is Amy Grace.
"A magical thing has happened,
"So rich, in this kitchen I inhabit.
"I heard a sound from the draining board
"But saw nothing there,
"Only transparency - I could see beyond the
wood.
"So I held out my hand,
"And -
"I felt a small creature's form,
"And fur-padded feet -
"Yet nothing, nothing seen.
"So I gathered it into my hands
"And - (her voice laughing)
"Felt it claw it's way onto my dress
"To nest between my shoulders and my face."

"My name", she says, "is Amy Grace."

"Good, good", smiled the headphones,
"Now my sweet, tell me more."

"She sleeps in a box beside my bed.
"She needs no food and takes no milk
"And no-one knows she is there but me.
"Sometimes she leaves her bed and comes to mine
"And I am Amy Grace.
"My fingers trace a small triangular face.
"I smooth the fine frill of her neck.

"Best of all, since she has no name,
"Since she is transparency
"She will never die."
"Thank you my sweet", said the headphones,
"Tikkety-boo and thank you, thank you
"And now who have we got?
"Julie from Beaulieu....."

Gallus gallus

The neighbour rooster set his gimlet eye
On the thin line of the eastern sky
The neighbour rooster opens up his beak
Time to speak- time to speak.

    Oo - Ah - Oo - Ah - Oo

A slid bolt frees the hen house door
And out they pour.

    Oo - Ah - Oo - Ah - Oo.

And where is she as the light lightens
And the day dawns cold?
Alone she stands. Alone! - and she's pure gold,
The plumage of her gilded drawers
Flows downward to her pretty claws.

    Oo - Ah - Oo - Ah - Oo

Favoured one, Princess Aida
See how delicately she pecks her due
My dainty feeder.

Oo - Ah - Oo - Ah - Oo

Yet my respects encompass all and sundry.
Her tiny eye grows eloquently thundery.
I avow the speckled procession
Is my profession.
The tiny eye grows warm.
For let me fail, I'm for the cooking pot
Hot!
Ha! How I wonder what her part will be,
A golden chick like her? A lad like me?
Or a four minute ovum for someone's tea?

Oo - Ah - Oo - Ah - Oo.

The Play

"Aldi Boronti Fosco Formio"
Chanted the Punch and Judy man.
The children ran, and the children ran.
And the play began.

"Oh I do like to be beside the seaside."
"What of the plot?" said the Punch and Judy
man
"Where have we got?
"Judy, Judy bring up the baby,
"Ikle, ikle baby,
"Tickle, tickle baby
"Biff, biff, biff."

A woman watched the running,
Heard the clamour
From a private hell and her personal war.
"That's the way to do it!" said the Punch and
Judy man.
But she saw the other baby hit the floor.

Murder and mayhem, mayhem and murder
Delicious villany fore and aft
And the innocent children laughed,
How they laughed.

And the woman walked away
She was no part of the Play.

Lugete O Veneres Cupidinesque.

She was one whose self- esteem was riven.
Ponderous solemn vows; what love given?
Forget who was sinned against and who sinning.
Go back to the beginning.

Apple cheeked hoyden with a fair mop;
Childish betrothed, showing her blue ring.
"I am honoured above everything."

Child bride in her honeymoon gear
Pink and pearled from breast to ear
With jaunty tricorne and ostrich plumes;
The gilded coach, the brave balloons.

Time the tyrant now takes over.
A boy is born a son and heir.
Later a while a brother, a spare.
Now she is firm in history
No mystery.

"Not enough. In my marriage there were
three.
He she and me."

And time gives her amazing charm.
"They want me to go quietly."
Then with a change of tone
"She will not go quietly."

On her island's quiet bed
Her shameless loveliness, all sped.
The lady lies dead.

Whatever is the feud of saint or sinner
Power always power is the winner.

Storms

Storm I

On that morning the sky
Delivered opaque sheets of rain;
Iron coloured, flooding the cellar
Through the road drain.
That ancient crucible the valley roof
Seeped a grey map on each bedroom ceiling
And set the wallpaper gently peeling.
The pines by the river took in
The geometric flights of lightening
And a thunderbolt took out chimneys
And their pots.
Then it was over.
The dun sky rolled back,
A few lances of lightning wavered and stayed
And shone like May on the wet world
Every droplet glancing.

Storm II

None knew why the lovely infant

Raised her voice in screaming, squared her
mouth,
Flailed her arms, threw herself flat
And held her breath and such as that,
Flung herself to the fireside mat
Refusing to be soothed and comforted
Sobbing, hiccupping, disarray
Such sorrow could go on all day.

Suddenly she sought
Strong arms and kisses
And ten minutes of love.
Then lifting a blue shod foot
Waving her hands in a precarious balance
She smiled sunbeams.
"Look", she said, "I dancing".

Laurie: Ode for a Happy Event

Laurence and Peter and Dan one day
Said "Time to be born and to learn how to play,
"And to walk and to think and to know what to
say."

So they went and got born - three into one
And the message went out "We have a son!
"Isn't it wonderful? Isn't it fun!"

"Isn't he lovely! Isn't he beautiful!
"Will he be loving? Will he be dutiful"
"As for our care of him? It will be suitable."

Laurence and Peter and Dan is here,
Tune up the voices; raise up a cheer,
Ring all the bells; rupture the steeple,
Tell all the dons.(And the ordinary people.)

Quite a small miracle, my little dear.
Laurence P. D.
Laurie for short, Lol for shorter!
Our son and heir
IS HERE.

Ode to Alistair

The little town of Eastleigh, of Eastleigh in
Hampshire
The little town of Eastleigh has nothing
much to show,
Except a splendid railtrack to venture and to
come back
And a neat small airfield where glad planes
go.
There are no dreaming spires there, nor yet a
steeple high
But rows of little houses between the earth
and sky.
But sleeping there in Eastleigh a little lovely
boy
(Again a father's pride, and again a mother's
joy)
With gentle brow unfurrowed beneath his
hazel hair
'Tis Alistair, but ten days old, lying sleeping
there.
What matter then the dons; what matters
then the steeple?
Alistair in Eastleigh is smiling for the people.
And dreamily, "A very vernal lad I am,
"I have come with the snowdrop
"I have come with the lamb."

Carol for a New Boy

Boy one felt sunshine hours
Boy two brought the lamb and flowers
Boy three cold November showers
Boy three sang this carol through the room
"Ego. Benedictus sum."

And his mother dreamy Jess
Whispered "Puer Benedictus es."
And the music of her smiling
Soft, loving, beguiling,
Honey warm, milk blest
Set mother, father,
Boys and all the people singing
"Gloria Benedictus est."

Nathaniel

Oh, dear my sire; Oh, dear my dam,
These wordlings tell you that I am
Filled to the brim with infant joy
That I am your midsummer boy.

Oxford birds are winging,
Oxford bells are ringing
And we three, we happy three
Are tuned and right for singing.

When you are old I'll be good to you
I'll bring you daisies and apples too.
I'll read you poems and write you stories
Making sure my love the more is.

The Oxford bells are ringing,
Oxford birds are winging
And now we three, we happy three
Together, will be singing.

Said the Baby

"I have tuned my little voice-box to a coo.
I have moved my rosebud lips to the air
And nothing gained but air.
I have hiccupped several times to no avail,
I am sad and solemn."
.......SAID THE BABY.

"My mother has not heard or
Having heard gives no response.
Before my late emergence
She would play me music by orchestra
Or cello or some such
And read me words by Keats:
'Oh what can ail thee.'
........SAID THE BABY.

"And swimming, diving, dancing,
I would certainly respond
And she would laugh her dear delicious
sound."
........SAID THE BABY.

"I thought the outside world would be all joy.
It is one long war.
I will wave my star-fish hands about,

Clench each tiny toe within my baby-grow,
Then I will whimper, cluck and sob,
Then I will bellow.
But only nicely
Because I am ABSOLUTELY LOVELY."
........SAID THE BABY.

Brown Man

I am brown man.
Long years ago I was brown boy
And my velvet eyes lit on
The daughter of a king. And she was fair.
I said "Cover her head. Cover her brazen
hair
And her arms and shoulders bare."
She was all ivory rose and gold.
With great pale eyes she looked through me.
No word was spoken,
My brown boy heart broken.

I am brown man.
My brother said "I will ease your pain,
And make you well again.
Let us make her a gift
A Maala village Dhow
In her hand to hold
With a silver deck and a prow of gold,
With shimmering sails too small for the sea."
And with deft hands he aided me.

We took it to her on a holy day
And again her pale eyes looked away.

I am a brown man. I am happy
For I am alive, the king's daughter is dead.
No more to be said.

Neighbour

Seven years she was my neighbour
I, next to her
She next to me.
A tall old woman in beetle black
With here or there a touch of colour;
Emerald, crimson, peacock blue.
She wore fine rings
Platinum and sapphire like pale water.
And on her dress a cartoon cat
Cut out of gold with diamond eyes.
And on her head a little hat
With an egret brush of feathers.

She called on me
"A dog is hoi polloi.
"A cat is an aristocrat.
"You will not throw hard things at my cats
"If they invade your lawn."
"I will make horrid noises,
"I may sprinkle water
"That also goes for my daughter."
She laughed then, "Come and have a drink
with me.
"When...I'm so busy. Oh-

"I'll let you know."
She came again when her fierce husband died.
Stood at the door. Would not come inside.
"He is dead and gone away
"What is there to say?
"My future is yesterday.
"You must have a drink with me,
"Sherry to make merry,
"Whiskey to make frisky -
"He should have said all this -
"Wine for feeling fine.
"I must go. I'll let you know!"

Later when friends came to tea with me,
She met them at the gate.
"I'm old and cold
"I'm blind, I'm deaf,
"No life, no fun, no good to anyone!"
They told me this after,
Falling about with laughter.

The last time I saw her
We walked together on green grass under a
wide tree.
"Why did you never have that drink with
me?
"It was not right- it was impolite.
"And who's the woman next to me?

"They tell me she's smart
"Writing, acting. Some kind of art.
"But is she gentry? That's going too far.
"They seldom if ever are."

On a gold autumn day, a white car
Came and took her away.
My neighbour left no trail
Except 'House for Sale'.

Invaders

They came in one by one
And two by two, whining and fussing,
To find the dish of plums
And smell the bubbling jam,
Plunged headlong into the sugary hell.

Make a trap; make it well
Take a paradise of juices sweet,
An ingress for them,
Some will find a moment's blissful
Drowning of a kind.
So many of them, striped invaders.

Do not brush them off, but let them crawl.
They want the plums, that is all.

The man came, a stocky man at noon
Carrying his haversack of doom.
"Go inside" he said, "Shut all access,
"I'll soon clear up this here mess,
"Wasps is dirty insects,
"Give me any time the friendly bee.
"Bees is clean."
He closed the door, shouted

"Don't come out, leave all to me
"There'll be poison about."
"But what of you?", I said.
"They won't come near", he said, "They fear
"The smell of strychnine,
"Oh, they fear the smell of this here."

From the windows I watch,
He fires at the wasp's fragile nest
Inside the nesting box.
The invaders make themselves into a cloud
Whining and buzzing loud,
And many fall to the dry grass.
I see a hundred make for home
Twist and spin and fall
And all the others rise like starlings
And turn towards the man.
He fires his gun again, drenching the nest.
And like a shower of rain
The wasps fall and do not rise again.
Long I watch the solitary wasps
Come, wheel and fly away.

"All right now", the man said as he goes
away,
"You're the third I've done today,
"Now you can get back to your jam.
"Afternoon, ma'am".

Sad to see the foragers come by,
Bewildered..... to home..... and die.

Night Thought

Between awake and asleep there is often
panoramic irrelevance.

The road. The gate. The gatehouse -
Cob walls, reeded roof.
Tapestry of a chairback.

First to the left - the Manor House,
A cubic place served by the farm
Where Charles two brought his new love.
They say she is seen in the maze
Weeping and inveighing,
For he has asked Nellie should be fed
And has forgotten her.

To the right the elms
And overhead the swarming stars and gib-
bous moon,
A velvet night - and a girl's voice saying
"I was afraid when the owl snored."
And of her own accord slipping her small dry
hand into mine,
Her cheek against my shoulder.
Ah, but her kiss was sweet

Her hair smelling of sun.
September night!
And the owl's silent flight.

Morning. The noise began.
Lowing cattle, shouting man.
Three turkey poults perched where the dripping
tap
Fed water to the brim of an old bath.
One bird fell in and drowned
No other looked around.

The woodman a living chainsaw
Calls out loud -
"Hickory wood for hammer handles. Ash for
window frames."
A shout, a cough, a wheeze,
"And mind out for they spiteful Italian bees".

Furzey Pound, set between two woods
Long and narrow -
Where a gypsy woman in a bender lived
On her own, old and alone.
A limb of sycamore bowed down,
It's tip embedded in the ground.
And there she lived.
Her smoke stained face
Brittle braids of hair strained by the years

Of daytime damp and night-time fears.
She moaned of "rheumatics", and on a day
Nathan, her son, took her away.

They - whoever were, decreed
Furzey Pound should be planted and treed
A thousand baby pines
In lines were left to grow - to be felled
For masts and poles. Not so -
Six inches high, the infant trees
Showed how to die - of calcin and disease.

The wheat - ripe for cutting
Shining as old gold
When the stag, facing the field as a tide
Swam a glittering swathe
Shaking, breaking the ears
His proud antlers - regal hatstands.
Gently it comes - no sudden leap
From wavering thought, the swing of sleep.

And two ride out -
The Don and his Esquire
The blood mare, no Rosinante,
And Sancho Panza on a sparkling bay
Breasting the day.
Where, oh where.................are the Windmills?

Old Woman

What does she think
The quiet woman
In the red chair in the nursing wing?
The charge nurse loves her
She makes no trouble
The tray bearers love her
She lends them her perfume and talcum
But what is she thinking
The quiet woman?

"Plymouth was a fine town
"When I was young in the sea and dancing
"When in thin china cups
"Came milkless tea at the tennis club
"And my mother wore a Leghorn hat
"With a red satin rose as big as this."

Shaping thin fingers to encircle air
That became the rose itself.

"Robert and I went each day
"To talk I think rather than play
"I wonder what became of him.

"His mother died.... I don't know what became
of him.
"He was a handsome boy."

She closes her eyes.

"There was another, older,
"I saw the whole world liquidise
"When people brought him to our house
"So much so I ran away.
"He followed. What had he to say?
"Like Romeo, his purpose marriage.
"We planned it so and he went back to sea.
"Slowly the houses turned to brick and stone
again.
"No regret; a little pain."

There must be more, dear quiet woman.

"I was a wife for sixty years or more
"And all that implies.
"Now I am random."

Old Woman II

Today again in the red chair.
Will she speak to me?

Coffee or tea?

She smiles denial.

"There was a winter wedding
"The bride icy in her bedgown
"Syringa white.
"He, pale from the drinking of the night.
"She, veiled and wreathed and given away.

Smiling.

"It is all unreal
"While sunlight bars from the bright win-
dows
"Stain her samite dressing
"With the primary colours of dead saints."

She is laughing silently.

"Was it your wedding?"

"I have forgotten.
"But the church was mine.
"Plymouth was a rare place
"When I was young.
"Oh, yes, I remember a wedding."

Her tray comes to her
But she is between lost and found.

"Were you happy?"

"Yes. I think so, when the children came
"All my lovely boys
"There was one who stroked the bees on the
lavender.
"One who was angel-voiced in singing.
"One who made a haven under the table
"To write his 'wisdom words'
"The others, younger, stumbling about in
play.
"But children come like flowers
"And in a little while they go away
"And strangers take there places.
"Some faces grow stronger
"With eyes less forgiving
"All my boys went away
"Children never stay ...."

"Oh, I am so tired - I am so tired.
"Remember what the poet said -
"I am marble - booted
"And gloved with lead."

Words

Manifestation? With sanction?

On Sunday words came through the walls;
The world's books it seemed
Spread and spreading, chopping, changing,
Spelling, miss-spelling,
Four 'e's in 'freedom'
And the long tails of 'y' and 'g'
Neat and sparing - drawn in old grey ink
With a steel school pen.

Then came the lines, four inches apart
Delicately parallel ceiling to floor.

"Look away my love", said I to myself;
Then quickly back to quench the movement.
But all was persistence.
Maybe traitorous eyes practised reflection?
Refraction? Reflection?
Phantom to mirage, mirage to phantom
The whole day.

On Monday the words are clean away

Though now and then the thin drawn lines
return.

Who will rid me?

Soliloquy

My mother saw an angel in 1934
Between the barn's roof timbers and the
threshing floor
She was full of Sunday school and heaven
She was seven
Her gentle father stroked her head
"Of course you saw an angel my love" he said
Her mother sent her supperless to bed.

"Tell me again of the angel
"Did he wear a halo and wings?"
"Oh no. He had much finer things
"He wore a long white bedgown
"That shimmered fold on fold
"His hands were made of silver
"His head was gold."

Oh I believed her angel
For none knew better than I
That miracles come with children.
"Mother, I could fly
"I flew down the steps to the wash-house
"And up the attic stair
"I would have flown the window
"If the glass had not been there."

My mother's face grew stony
Her icy eyes met mine.
"You fell down the steps to the wash-house
"You climbed the attic stair
"You dreamed the glassy window,
"For there is no window there.
"Please tell me nothing more"
I wept. "Mother, I was only four."

The ending of the story:
Mother keeps her golden glory,
So it must seem.
I, a climb, a dream, a bruising fall,
No father's hand to stroke my head.
And that is all.

The Inevitable

The yellow house in Bedfordshire
They called 'The Creaking Stair'
Each in a solemn secrecy
The ladies settled there.

Mary, Phyllis, Doris, Cora,
April, May, June and Nora.
Kathleen,Mabel, Ethel, Thora,
Hilda, Millicent and Dora;
Linked together in that house,
Never a spider, never a mouse,
Here a pretty little dog
And there a cat - a sweet, sweet mog -
And all these ladies were old as old
And all these ladies were good as gold.

Would these ladies die quite soon?
To be scattered under sun and moon?
All these ladies old as old
Behind each one a tale untold.
And each would scuttle off to bed
Holding a volume read, unread-
Thinking, perhaps of things 'He'd' said.
But all these ladies now are dead.

A Life

"Edwin... Ah, my son, my son!"
(He was my father, granny's youngest one.)
First the wedding to the red-haired George.
Then the seven girls....the names....now,
Annie, Lucy, Jessie, Sue.... then another two,
Kate and Nellie, followed Millie.
Six years of rest
Then William ... "My son Billy"
And Edwin, "Ah, my son, my little son!"
"My little, pretty boy"...date 1884
And by heaven's grace, no more.
The seven sisters loved him.
And when Jessie died
Susie took him to the coffin's side, aged three,
To kiss and say goodnight.
And taught him "poor Jessie dead,
Poor Jessie cold." And he but three years old,
With sandy curling hair
And grey green stare.

The sisters loved him,
Father chastised him.
His mother wept, "Oh, Edwin, my son, my son."
And Billy, well aware,

That all was not quite fair.
"Give me that 'Go-been'!"
"No, that my 'Go-been'!'
"Give me that 'Go-been' or you'll go away to
green."
And sobbing, Edwin gives away
His toy, he fashioned yesterday.
A piece of wood, a little raft,
Billy took it. Billy laughed.

Tyrant time took over.
Annie to a lover.
Two to marriage,
Nell to early death.
Susan to St Barts (breaker of hearts).
Tyrant time took over.
The home, a strange disordered scene
And Edwin just fourteen.

"What shall we do with Edwin?"
("Oh, my son, my son!")
Schoolmaster called.
"You have a clever boy
He is lazy and uncaring
And your rod, sir, unsparing.
He has much of mischief, not of sin
You say you hope to beat the devil out.

But I fear you have beaten
Deception and anger in.
Now he is fourteen and his childhood done."

Weeping "Oh, Edwin, my son, my son!"
But red-haired George, more sandy now,
Took little heed.
Indeed, he beat the boy.
Then on a day Edwin seized the cane,
Broke it and threw it away.
His mother smiled, "Edwin, my son"

The family speaks:

1924 Billy

Edwin? Oh! You mean my brother -
We called him Neddy.
Or sometimes Johnny
A nice enough fellow
He would be forty now.
A soft one he was,
I could get anything from him
With a threat that he'd "go away to green".
You know - a sixpence, a florin
His stamps, Empire and foreign.
I don't deny he'd cry.

Between us Father and I gave him hell.
Ah! Well!
He became a good athlete
A sprinter - very fleet.
He won clocks and watches.
I must away - busy day.

1924 Susan

You asked about Edwin
The baby brother - forty now.
He was so lovely.
Mischievous of course,
Cruelly punished, often beaten,
But who could gainsay George?
I don't care if Neddy seemed undutiful
He was so beautiful.

1934 Margaret, His Wife

You ask about my husband?
One of his friends?
One of those failures who make amends?
I asked my husband once
"Who are your friends?"
He merely shook his head
"Their name is legion", Edwin said.

2001 His Daughter

I think my father was a good man
But always out of time and place.
He was well read
Followed false gods
Joined lost causes
Supported anti-heroes
Was once dismissed his ship.
I think he never learned to love.
Small wonder you will say,
For in his earliest time
Those who said they loved him
One by one drifted away,
Leading to contempt of father and brother
And the iron frailty of his mother
Who birthed him at forty one
And died at eighty nine.
Some loved Edwin, unconsidered people,
Writing sad letters when he died.
I did not love him then
And now it is too late.
I understand you now Edwin, my father.

Sister Millie

Millie was pretty, very pretty
Everything Millie said because she was pretty,
was witty.
With her sandy hair
Her aquamarine eyes
She was a prize.
Like Annie, but half the size
From her tiny gloves
To her size three shoes
She had an eye for Frank
So patent leather his healthy hair,
So spandy smart his suits
So yellow his dog skin gloves
So bright his hand-made boots.
Yet Frank was not a Boulevardier
But a sorrowing widower.
So she was kind to him
She gentled him dear Millie!
Dressed so frilly
And daffo down dilly.
She took his gentle hand
Into her hand.
"Mother" she said, "I married him,
The Christian thing to do."

Her mother said
"My sole regret is that
Your lovely husband
Who is a jeweller with a cottage,
Is not brand new."

Sister Annie

She was as trim as a daisy
Sweet as a bee
Her to and fro-ing
Coming and going
Gleam and glow
Were a pleasure to see.
Yet one fine day she vanished away
None knew why - or did not say.
From the loft there went a valise
And from the press
Cambric nightgowns and drawers
A rose-printed dress
And a small hat with a pink flower
The little tippet of squirrel fur,
Elizabeth Barrett Browning's sonnets,
Her own and Jessie's baby bonnets.
(Jessie dead six months past
Pale in life as pale at the last.)
The parents stormed but none would tell
What someone must have known quite well.
In reply to the question the mother said
"She has gone to be a lady's maid."
No one was satisfied,
Interest flagged, then died.

Annie was seen in Manchester,
Chester le Street, Ilchester,
Romsey, Salcombe, Ivybridge,
Half a dozen other places
Anywhere to save their faces.
Telling all - never:
Annie was gone forever.

POEMS TO READ ALOUD